CONTENTS

D1080769

Some words are shown in bold, **like this**. You can find out what they mean by looking in the glossary.

HOW DID WORLD WAR I CHANGE WOMEN'S LIVES?

In August 1914, the nations of Europe stumbled into the biggest war in their history. Huge armies from the **Allies**, including Great Britain, France, and Russia, faced the **Central Powers** of Germany and **Austria-Hungary**. Nations outside Europe were sucked into the conflict, including British **dominions** such as Australia, India, and Canada, several British **colonies**, and, in 1917, the United States.

The war did not just change the lives of the men in the armies. Women's lives and place in society changed, too, as every part of society pulled together to try to win the war. Women played a vital part in the war effort as they took on jobs that men had previously done, from driving buses to working on farms.

As husbands, fathers, and sons went off to fight the enemy, millions of women were left to care for families and households on their own.

ON THE FRONT LINE

Many women went further and **volunteered** to help at the front line. Some even took roles that put them directly in the line of fire. By the time the war finished, women's place in society had changed forever. To understand what this meant, we need to understand women's lives in the years before 1914.

Before the war, jobs such as mending gas stoves would have been done by men.

In their own words

"I think we may write it down in history that on August 4th, 1914 the door of the Doll's House opened – For the shot that was fired in Serbia [at the start of the war] summoned men to their most ancient occupation – and women to every other."

Mabel Potter Daggett, American journalist, writing during the war

WHAT WAS LIFE LIKE FOR WOMEN BEFORE THE WAR?

In 1900, most women lived quite restricted lives by today's standards. After leaving school in their early teens, working-class young women would be expected to go out to work. In Britain, 2 million women worked in industry, although the number of women workers in other countries such as Germany was much lower. Once they got married, women would usually stay at home to look after children. Managing a home was a big job with none of the **labour-saving** appliances, such as washing machines, that we take for granted today.

Working class women would often work as cooks and servants in the houses of wealthier families.

DID YOU KNOW?

In 1900, over 1.5 million British women worked as **domestic servants**, but there were only two qualified female architects.

Rich women like this Russian aristocrat had few opportunities to find out about the world outside their high society.

Women in the upper classes had more leisurely lives but they were not much more independent than working women. Their lives were mapped out with a series of social events, while the world of business and power was left to men. Many men believed that a woman's place was in the home.

EDUCATION

However, by 1900, things were starting to change, particularly for women from richer families. Women made up a growing proportion of college students in many countries. In the United States, nearly half of all students were women. However, even educated women found it difficult to be accepted in professional jobs, such as medicine.

British suffragettes campaigning for the vote before World War I.

HUNGER FOR CHANGE

Women who were educated or working in similar jobs to men, often with much less pay, wanted the same rights as men. One of the most disputed areas was the right to vote. Women could vote in national elections in New Zealand (1893) and Australia (1902) and in some elections elsewhere, such as in many US states. In most national elections, women did not have a vote.

SUFFRAGETTES

In the early 1900s, groups of women, as part of an international **suffrage** movement, campaigned fiercely for political rights. In Britain, Emmeline Pankhurst and her daughter Christabel co-founded the Women's Social and Political Union. Members of this union became known as the suffragettes. Women were sent to jail for increasingly violent protests. Some, such as Emily Davison, who threw herself in front of the king's horse at the Derby horse race, even died for their cause. American campaigners, including Alice Paul and Clara Burns, learned from the British suffragettes in their own campaign for the vote.

The outbreak of war brought an end to the suffragettes' campaign. No one knew what the future held as millions of men went off to fight. Whatever happened, women were determined to be at the heart of the war effort.

Susan B. Anthony and Elizabeth Cady Stanton campaigned for the vote in the United States. Their tactics were less extreme than the suffragettes.

In their own words

"Life was so normal ..., and this was something that threw everybody out of gear. Our friends – boyfriends – were rushing to join up. It was changing our lives completely."

Ruby Ord, who was eighteen when war broke out in 1914

"Powerless though we are politically, we call upon the governments and powers of our several countries to avert the threatened unparalleled disaster."

A plea from the International Woman Suffrage Alliance sent to governments and embassies a few days before the outbreak of war

WHAT DID WOMEN DO ON THE HOME FRONT?

The war transformed life in all the warring countries, even if they were far away from the actual fighting. The industries and people who helped the war effort were all part of the home front. Most people were enthusiastic about the war. In Britain, men rushed to volunteer for the army. The government tried to persuade women to encourage their husbands and boyfriends to volunteer. Most other countries did not need volunteers to expand their already large armies.

At the start of the war, women's roles were still very limited. British women formed groups to support the troops, such as the Victoria League and the Active Service League. They pledged never to be seen in public with a man who had "refused to respond to his country's call".

DID YOU KNOW?

Women were encouraged to help by knitting warm clothes for those at the front. These were not always gratefully received. One soldier wrote to his mother that many of these were "thin and shoddy" compared to the clothing sent out by the government.

THE REALITY OF WAR

On mainland Europe, the war had a much more immediate impact on women. As Germany invaded Belgium and northern France, whole families were forced to flee for their lives. The vast French and German forces suffered hundreds of thousands of **casualties** in the first weeks of war. Soldiers' wives and mothers had to face the pain of losing loved ones.

In their own words

"... what a chapter of horrors! How much blood, death, destruction! Each day we hear of new victims. In our district one poor woman who has six sons in uniform, has just learned that four are dead!"

Louise Delétang, a worker in Paris, recalls the shock of war in August 1914

Belgian refugees receive meals from a Dutch relief committee at the market square in Bergen op Zoom, Netherlands.

Before the war, French women would not have been seen operating lathes.

GOING TO WORK

The war years saw a huge change in the work that women were expected to do outside the home. Women had worked before the war, but now they were taking on jobs very different from their traditional roles as domestic servants, nurses, and teachers.
In the first months of the war, many women who worked in industry actually lost their jobs as the uncertain times led to businesses closing factories or cutting staff. Organizations such as the British Queen's Work for Women Fund were set up to give work to women affected by **unemployment**. The war soon created new jobs in industry.

In Germany, women soon took on dangerous jobs, such as making fuses for hand grenades.

MAKING MUNITIONS

In France, women were not allowed to work in **munitions** factories making **shells** and weapons for the war, but Germany quickly employed women in this dangerous work. In 1915, Britain's women began to take on these essential jobs. Pay was good in the munitions factories, but the work was hard, with long hours and night shifts in unheated factories.

In their own words

"We were making something that was going to kill or maim others... They were youngsters just coming up in life like I was, sixteen or seventeen. They had parents too. That made me feel sad sometimes."

Florence Nield was one of many munitions workers troubled by the deadly purpose of their work

Emmeline Pankhurst (1858-1928)

British activist Emmeline Pankhurst made her name as one of the leaders of the suffragette movement before the war. During the war, she campaigned for "Women's Right to Serve", believing that women could do more than knitting and nursing. She urged industries to employ women and release men to serve in the forces. She also travelled to the United States, Canada, and Russia to spread the same message.

DID YOU KNOW?

In 1918, a British government survey found that the number of women with jobs had increased from 5.9 million to 7.3 million, but the type of job had changed with fewer domestic servants.

NEW JOBS FOR WOMEN

Women were not new to factories, but there were many areas of work where women had not been seen before. At the time, there were no laws forcing businesses to treat men and women equally.

In Paris, France, women were working as conductors on trams. Most countries required all men to join the forces, so they needed women workers in all sorts of areas from the start of the war. British men were not **conscripted** until 1916, so women took over their jobs more gradually.

Transport was one area where women workers found new jobs in many countries. Office jobs had been traditionally filled by men, but these were also attractive to women. As more and more men were called away to the war, women also found jobs in heavy industry, such as shipbuilding.

SERVANT SHORTAGE

Some wealthy women had to learn new skills, such as cooking and cleaning for themselves. The number of other jobs available meant domestic servants were in short supply.

Pankhurst was inspired when she saw women driving trams in Paris, France.

Farm work was hard, particularly as many horses were needed for the war effort. However, all nations needed to grow as much food as they could.

DID YOU KNOW?

In 1916, it was discovered that there were fewer women working on the land than before the war. This change happened because the war had created other jobs that paid workers more money.

ON THE LAND

One of the biggest needs was for women to work on farms. Blockades by ships made it very difficult for countries, particularly those in central Europe, to bring in food from overseas. Farms had an essential role to play in the war. Sometimes this meant wives and children taking on the family farm, but governments also **recruited** women to work on farms.

British women were recruited into the Women's Forage Corps or the Women's Land Army. The American Women's Land Army was started in 1917, when the United States entered the war. It brought 20,000 women from towns and cities to work on US farms, which were so important to the Allied war effort. In Germany, Belgian and Polish prisoners were often forced to work on farms.

WORKING LIFE

Life was not always easy for women working in jobs that had previously been done by men. Women who worked in factories or as bus conductors sometimes found the men they worked with were unfriendly. They were clearly not convinced that women could do the job just as well as their male colleagues who were away fighting.

In their own words

"Some people tell me that I shall not be able to go on with my farm work in the winter, because it will make my hands so bad. But I intend to stick to it. Our men don't stop fighting in the cold weather, and neither shall I."

A letter from Dorothy Chalmers, who worked on a farm in the Midlands during the war

HOW DID WOMEN CARE FOR THE WOUNDED?

Nursing was one area where women were already well established. Nurses such as Florence Nightingale had tended the wounded in previous wars. Nurses in World War I, many of whom were young volunteers with only basic training, faced huge challenges due to the numbers of casualties and the horrific injuries they had to treat.

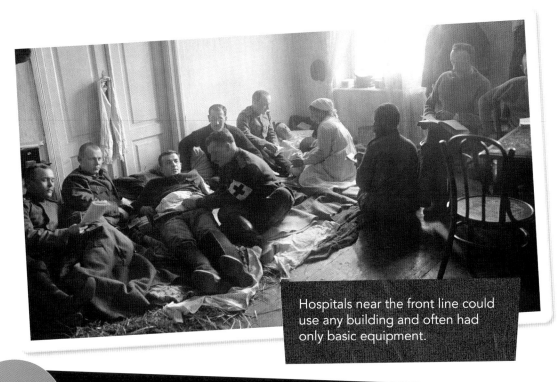

Hospitals near the front line could use any building and often had only basic equipment.

WHO'S WHO?

Elsie Knocker (1884–1978) and Mairi Chisholm (1896–1981)

British ambulance drivers Elsie Knocker and Mairi Chisholm started a first aid station in a cellar close to the Belgian front in August 1914. They were often shelled as they picked wounded soldiers up from the muddy battlefield. In 1918, they were **gassed** in a German attack and had to return home. Their bravery and success in saving lives earned them many medals.

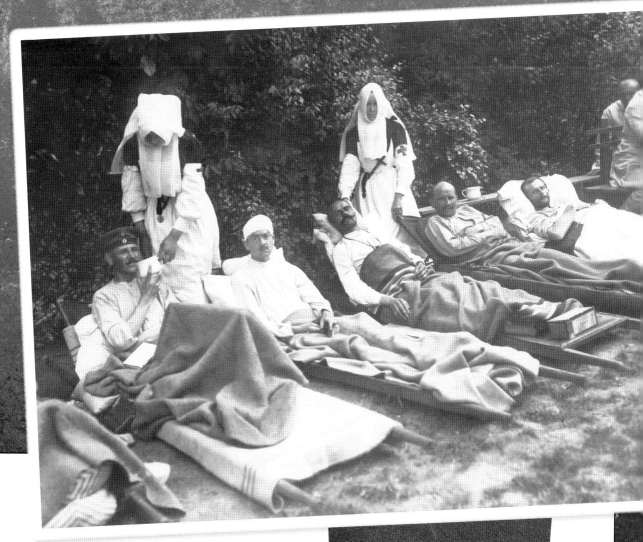

Nuns tend to wounded German soldiers in the garden of an army hospital in France.

NURSING AT THE FRONT

Wounded soldiers were first treated at first aid stations behind the front line. They were then moved to field hospitals further from the fighting and, if necessary, by train or ship closer to their homes. Nurses working close to the fighting faced great danger.

DID YOU KNOW?

At the start of the war, women were discouraged from medical work close to the front line. Scottish doctor Elsie Inglis volunteered to lead an ambulance unit and was told to "go home and sit still"! Another woman doctor in France was told by a senior officer, "I don't know anything about lady doctors. Do you bite?"

EVEN MORE NURSES

Between 1914 and 1918, the number of female British military nurses increased from 2,600 to more than 18,000. Other countries saw similar changes. The US Army Nurse Corps had 21,480 members by 1918. More than 2,000 nurses from the Australian Army Nursing Services also served overseas during the war, mostly in Europe and the Middle East.

AMBULANCES AT THE FRONT

The British Voluntary Aid Detachment (VAD) and First Aid Nursing Yeomanry (FANYs) formed before the war. The VADs included men and women but, during the war, most male volunteers were fighting at the front. The VADs and FANYs worked as nurses and ambulance drivers at the front, particularly after 1915. In 1917, the National League for Women's Service was formed in the United States, based on the structure of the British VADs.

In their own words

"One day I saw this young man on a stretcher. It was my brother, so I said to the soldiers who were carrying him: 'Put him in my ambulance, I am his sister.' When he died the next day I was with him, holding his hand."

Catherine Cathcart-Smith, who drove an ambulance collecting wounded soldiers when they arrived by train in London

The ambulance drivers often came from the wealthier classes as they could already drive. Motorized ambulances were used for the first time during the war. Ambulance drivers at the front had to do their work under fire from enemy artillery. Others had to collect horribly wounded soldiers from trains and take them to hospital.

These British volunteers are learning to drive their ambulance before being sent to France.

WHO'S WHO?

Marie Curie (1867–1934)

Polish-born physicist and chemist Marie Curie was the first woman to win a Nobel Prize and one of the most remarkable scientists in history. When war broke out, Curie pioneered the use of X-rays from her home in Paris. X-ray machines could save lives by helping doctors to see bullets, shrapnel, and broken bones. She equipped a fleet of ambulances with mobile X-ray machines and often drove them herself to the battle zones.

ON OTHER FRONTS

Dr Elsie Inglis and the other leaders of the Scottish Women's Hospitals had been part of the suffragette movement before the war. After the British Army decided they didn't need them, Inglis and her team set up a hospital in France. They also set up units on every front in the war from Malta to Russia. Inglis was captured when the Central Powers invaded Serbia. Meanwhile, most of her nurses were forced to flee enemy attacks with the Serbian Army across the icy mountains of Albania.

Women at the Scottish Women's Hospital were expected to show discipline and follow the orders of their leader Dr Elsie Inglis.

In their own words

"There was no longer a defined way; the whole earth was now an untrodden track... Whichever way you looked, oxen, horses, and human beings were struggling, and rolling, and stumbling, all day long in ice and snow."

Muriel St Clair Stobart describes the Scottish Women's Hospital's journey through the mountains of Albania during the Great Retreat of Serbian forces in 1915

WOMEN IN CHARGE

While women doctors were still rare in the war, the Women's Hospital Corps, led by Flora Murray and Louisa Garrett Anderson, ran military hospitals in France and an all-women hospital in London. Newspaper reports said that at first the hospital "was viewed with suspicion", but this soon changed when patients saw the work of the women doctors. This was just one of the many hospitals on the home front, staffed by thousands of volunteers.

These American nurses are awaiting duty. When the United States entered the war in 1917, there were just 403 nurses on active duty. By 1918, there were more than 12,000.

DID WOMEN FIGHT IN THE WAR?

Women's bravery and determination was shown in many areas of the war effort, from the front line hospitals to the dangerous munitions factories. Few women actually fought in the war but there were many times when women put themselves in danger, often with terrible consequences.

EDITH CAVELL

One of the most famous victims of the war was British nurse Edith Cavell. She was executed by the Germans after she confessed to releasing wounded British prisoners of war from the Red Cross hospital in Brussels, where she worked. US and Spanish authorities had tried to prevent the execution. For many people, the German action confirmed Allied stories about the evil enemy they were fighting.

Edith Cavell helped around 200 Allied soldiers to escape from Belgium before her arrest in 1915.

The shattered towns of the **Western Front** forced many women who lived there to protect themselves and their families.

Women such as Edith Cavell and Emilienne Moreau were just the best-known examples of women involved at the front line in wartime. There were certainly many more individual stories of women who helped both sides, such as by spying or passing information about the enemy's troops or plans.

SUPPORTING MILITARY FORCES

Many of the office jobs that women now filled were directly connected to the war itself, whether in the giant government departments that managed the war in all countries, or in more specialized services such as military intelligence. In France, the government administration grew by a quarter between 1914 and 1918.

As casualties rose and more men were needed to serve at the front, governments tried to bring more women in to serve in support roles for the military, such as answering telephones, administrative work, and cooking meals. In Britain, the Women's Army Auxiliary Corps (WAAC) was created in 1917. They wore khaki uniforms and were organized in ranks similar to the regular armed forces. The Women's Royal Navy Service was set up in January 1918.

These women gardeners of the WAAC are tending the graves of fallen soldiers on the Western Front in France.

Back our girls over there

Y.W.C.A.

United War Work Campaign

Outside the British forces, women found it even more difficult to join the military. Canadian women were trained to fight on the home front, but did not serve overseas. Even the United States, which sent thousands of nurses to France in 1917, refused to use women in office roles in France. One of the few exceptions were the 300 "Hello Girls" of the Army Signal Corps, who served in France as telephone operators, speaking French and English.

Telephones were cutting-edge technology in 1917, but each call had to be connected by an operator.

In their own words

"After we were married, my husband wrote for my victory medal, as he was always proud of my service. They wrote back that I wasn't entitled to it, and that was the first time that I knew I wasn't in the army."

Merle Egan-Anderson served in the Signal Corps and was shocked to discover she was not a member of the army, despite having to follow military regulations

WOMEN IN BATTLE

Women who actually fought alongside their male comrades were very unusual in World War I. Dorothy Lawrence, a young British woman, spent several days in **trenches** on the Western Front after disguising herself and using false papers as Private Denis Smith. Flora Sandes was a vicar's daughter from Suffolk, England, who fought in some of the war's most brutal battles. She travelled to Serbia in 1914 as a nurse, but fought alongside Serbian forces as they were forced to retreat from their own country in 1915. Sandes found it difficult to return to the traditional role expected of women when she returned from the war.

Flora Sandes was known as "our Joan of Arc" by the Serbians, after the famous French heroine.

DID YOU KNOW?

There were many acts of individual heroism and bravery. Frenchwoman Marcelle Semmer held back a German advance by opening a canal lock and throwing away the key so German forces could not cross the canal. The British general who later controlled the area ordered his men to salute Semmer whenever they saw her.

"WOMEN'S DEATH BATTALION"

The only all-women fighting force in the war was the Women's Battalion of the Russian Army. When their leader Maria Bochkareva called for recruits in May 1917 "to dry the tears and heal the wounds of Russia", 2,000 women joined the battalion in the final months of Russia's war.

Maria Bochkareva (first from right above) hoped that her women's battalion would inspire Russia's men to keep fighting.

WHO'S WHO?

Maria Bochkareva (1889–1920)

The leader of the Battalion of Death came from a peasant family. She joined the Russian Army in 1914 and impressed the men with her bravery in battle, during which she was wounded twice. As well as fighting in World War I, Bochkareva's soldiers also fought against Russia's new **communist** leaders. She was captured and executed in 1920, during Russia's **civil war**.

WHAT CHALLENGES DID WOMEN FACE AT HOME?

While many women found new challenges in work, nursing, or other roles during the war, most married women still had to cope with running a household and family at the same time. Many homes during World War I did not even have running water, let alone the many other appliances that we take for granted today. Women did not just have to deal with separation from husbands and sons who were fighting, and the knowledge that they might never return. Rising prices and shortages of food and other items led to **rationing**, making home life even more difficult.

Queuing for basic food was a daily problem for women during the war.

KEEPING IN TOUCH

Soldiers at the front relied on letters to bring them news from home and relieve the boredom of days spent in the trenches between attacks. Letters were supposed to reassure the men that all was well at home, so many women kept any problems they had to themselves.

European soldiers might get a few days leave at home, giving them just enough time to get clean and rest before they returned to the horror of war. For soldiers from further afield, such as the many Australians serving in Europe, even this small time at home was not possible.

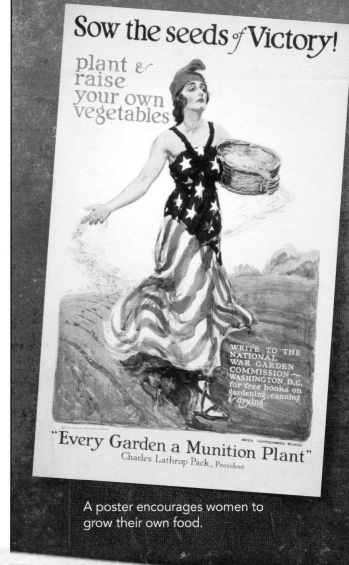

A poster encourages women to grow their own food.

In their own words

"All that day he was tired — he only got six days leave and he'd spent two of them travelling, so he didn't have very long. But the next day he said to me, 'Now Kitty, what would you like for a present? I'm going to buy you a present while I'm home.'... Anyway, he went back on the Thursday night... And it seems he told his friend, 'I'm afraid I shall never come back again.'"

Kitty Eckersley's husband comes home on leave

FREEDOM AND INDEPENDENCE

Although the separation and uncertainty of war made life difficult for many women, others found that war brought freedom and independence. This was particularly true of young unmarried women who did not have to look after a family, or women from wealthier backgrounds who had tasted the world of work for the first time.

As women's jobs changed, so did their clothes, with trousers and shorter hairstyles becoming popular.

DID YOU KNOW?

The Women's Institute started in rural Canada. The organization came to Britain in 1915 as a way of encouraging country women to grow and preserve food. It currently has more than 200,000 members.

Many of these women had more money in their pockets than before the war. A young woman from Belfast got paid six times her previous wages when she moved to a munitions factory in England. However, women were usually paid less than men doing the same job.

SPENDING MONEY

Shortages meant there were limits about what women could spend their money on. Nights at the cinema and dancing were popular. Clothing too was less restricted. Trousers and shorter hairstyles were more practical for many of the new jobs that women took on.

In their own words

"The wartime business girl is to be seen any night dining out alone or with a friend in the moderate-priced restaurants in London. Formerly she would never have had her evening meal in town unless in the company of a man friend."

A report from the Daily Mail newspaper, April 1916

Young women without children had more time for relaxing, like these swimmers.

OPPOSING THE WAR

One woman, when asked what she did in the war, replied that she spent the war trying to stop it. Although many women made a contribution to fighting the war, women also made up some of the conflict's strongest opponents. Men who campaigned against the war were dismissed as cowards who did not want to fight themselves. Women were able to voice their opposition, even if their views were often unpopular.

Alice Wheeldon (right) is pictured here with her daughters, Hettie and Winnie, and their prison warden (left) as they await trial.

WHO'S WHO?

Alice Wheeldon (1866–1919)

Wheeldon was a suffragette and peace campaigner who started a network to help British **conscientious objectors** who refused to fight in the war. In 1917, Wheeldon was sentenced to 10 years in prison for a supposed plot to kill the prime minister, although she was released a few months later. The evidence was probably invented because Wheeldon had sheltered people who opposed the war.

Many women anti-war campaigners came from the suffragette movement, although other suffragettes, such as Emmeline Pankhurst, supported the war. Women raised money and provided shelter for men who refused to fight in the war.

INTERNATIONAL OPPOSITION

The votes for women campaign included groups in many different countries, and they were able to organize an international movement against the war, with conferences in Switzerland and the Netherlands in 1915. Allied women who supported the war criticized the conferences and said they were the work of German agents.

These wartime bus workers are campaigning for equal pay with men.

Women also took part in action to improve their conditions in the war. In 1917, while French soldiers mutinied on the Western Front, the women of Paris went on strike for better pay and shorter working hours. The Russian **Revolution** of March 1917 actually started from a protest by women to mark International Women's Day.

WHAT HAPPENED TO WOMEN AT THE END OF WORLD WAR I?

At the start of 1918, there were around 6,000 women of the British WAAC stationed in France. As American men were conscripted into the military, American women found new opportunities for work. Nurses from the United States had been some of the first Americans to arrive on the Western Front after the country declared war in April 1917.

African American men and women from the southern states, who faced greater obstacles and **prejudice** than white women, travelled to cities such as New York and Chicago to find work by the end of the war.

Women were able to join the US Naval Reserve for the first time during World War I.

In their own words

"In the ultimate analysis, it is the nation with the best women that's going to win this war."

Count Johann von Bernstorff, German Ambassador to the United States, 1916

STRAIN OF WAR

By 1918, the strain of war was taking its toll on women. Many in Germany and Austria-Hungary were starving, and millions of women were grieving for loved ones or facing life after the war with a seriously wounded man. In Britain, there were no longer enough women coming forward to fill the available jobs, so teenagers and children started to work instead or as well as going to school.

As more men were conscripted into the forces, teenage girls often went to work in factories.

AFTER THE WAR

Most people were not expecting the war to end when it did. The news of the **armistice** on 11 November 1918 was met with a mixture of relief and celebration in cities like London, New York, and Paris. The people of Germany and Austria-Hungary faced revolutions, so the end of the war was less significant than the continuing dangers they faced. Civil war also raged in Russia.

When the celebrations died down, many women were only too happy to leave the world of work. They had taken jobs during the war because of poverty or a wish to help the war effort.

Others needed to work and faced competition for jobs from millions of men returning from the war. As a result, women often lost their jobs to the returning men. There were campaigns for single and widowed women to have priority in the jobs that remained, ahead of married women.

DID YOU KNOW?

In Britain, the number of women doing paid work increased by 1.6 million between 1914 and 1918. Only 2.3 million women worked in Germany in 1918, but this was a big increase from 1.5 million in 1914. The number of American women employed in industry increased by two and a half times between 1917 and 1918. Many of these women returned to home life within a few months of the war ending.

In their own words

"Put the married women out, send them home to clean their houses and look after the man they married and give a mother's care to their children. Give the single women and widows the work."

Letter from Isobel Pazzey to the British Daily Herald newspaper, October 1919

Members of the Royal Australian Naval Service celebrate the armistice in London.

VOTES FOR WOMEN

The war had interrupted women's campaign to have a vote in national elections. The actions of suffragettes had made sure that people knew about their campaign, but it had turned many people against the cause. During the war, many women's rights campaigners had worked for peace, but others had supported the war and the part women played in it.

CHAOS IN EUROPE

For many of Europe's women, the end of the war did not bring peace. Although women were allowed to vote in revolutionary Russia, the country was split by civil war, so it counted for little. Other countries also faced revolution. A short-lived communist revolution in Germany was led by a woman – Rosa Luxemburg.

WHO'S WHO?

Rosa Luxemburg (1871–1919)

Born in Poland, Luxemburg was the joint leader of the Spartacus League who had planned a revolution to end the war. She was murdered by police after attempting to seize power in Berlin in the weeks after the war.

GETTING THE VOTE

In 1918, women were finally given the right to vote in many countries, including Germany and Canada. In Britain, this was limited to women over the age of 30, while all men over 21 were given the vote. American women gained the right to vote in 1920. French women had to wait another 25 years before they were given the vote in 1944.

These major steps on the road to political equality may have happened without women's role in the war. However, the war had undoubtedly seen big steps towards equality in many other areas of women's lives, even if there was still a long way to go.

In the election of December 1918, British women voted for the first time.

REMEMBERING THE WOMEN OF WORLD WAR I

Many of the women who lived through World War I found that their lives were changed forever by the terrible conflict. Around 10 million soldiers died in the war. More than half of them were between the ages of 20 and 29.

Most of the casualties of war were men. However, incidents such as air raids and explosions in munitions factories also claimed women's lives. Many more women were affected by starvation and conflict in central Europe and Russia. Moreover, women across all the warring nations were left to pick up the pieces of their broken families.

The sacrifice of one woman was remembered when crowds lined the streets of London for the funeral procession of Nurse Edith Cavell in 1919 (see page 24).

SYMBOL OF REMEMBRANCE

Today, many people remember the dead of World War I and all wars since then by wearing poppies around Remembrance Day on 11 November, the day the war ended. Poppies grew in the fields of Belgium where many of the bloodiest battles took place. American YWCA worker Moina Michaels first sold silk poppies to support veterans in the United States. Frenchwoman Anna Guerin started making poppies and introduced the idea to Britain in 1921. The symbol was soon adopted in Australia, Canada, and New Zealand.

In their own words

"You thought about all the people you had known who were killed. They were just in the war zone and they could come home in your imagination. But the Armistice brought the realization to you that they weren't coming back, that it was the end."

Ruby Ord, a WAAC member who served in France during the Great War

Today, women like this US Marine serve alongside men in war zones around the world.

TIMELINE

1893	New Zealand becomes the first country to allow women to vote, followed by Australia in 1902
1909	Voluntary Aid Detachments are formed in Britain, including both men and women

1914

28 July–4 August	War is declared, beginning with Austria-Hungary declaring war on Serbia and ending with the British declaring war on Germany
August	Elsie Knocker and Mairi Chisholm start their first aid station on the Western Front

1915

January	British women first employed as munitions workers in factories
18 April	Women from Europe and the United States meet in the Hague, Netherlands, at the International Congress of Women, to call for an end to the war
23 May	Italy enters the war on the Allied side
12 October	Germany executes British nurse Edith Cavell
November	Scottish Women's Hospital begin retreat across Albanian mountains with Serbian troops

1916

21 February	Battle of Verdun begins
25 May	Universal conscription introduced in Britain, meaning that women are needed to take over many jobs
1 July	Beginning of the Battle of the Somme, with 57,000 British troops killed or wounded on the first day
1 December	Women's Auxiliary Army Corps (WAAC) formed in Britain

1917

January	National League for Women's Service formed in the United States
19 January	Many munitions workers are killed in an explosion at the Silvertown munitions factory in London
8 March	"February Revolution" in Russia leads to the end of the reign of Tsar Nicholas II and to a new government in Russia
31 July	Battle of Passchendaele, also known as the Third Battle of Ypres, begins
6 April	The United States declares war on Germany
May	Maria Bochkareva sets up the Women's Battalion in Russia

1918

21 March	German spring offensive begins, pushing Allied forces into retreat
10 June	Representation of the People Act changes British law to allow women over 30 to vote
11 November	Armistice agreed to end the war at 11.00 a.m. on the 11th day of the 11th month

After the war

14 December 1918	General Election in Great Britain. Women over 30 vote for the first time.
29 November 1919	Lady Nancy Astor becomes the first British woman Member of Parliament
26 August 1920	Nineteenth Amendment to US Constitution gives American women the right to vote in national elections

GLOSSARY

Allies countries fighting together against the Central Powers, including the empires of France, Russia, and Great Britain, and later the United States

armistice agreement to stop fighting

Austria-Hungary former European monarchy made up of Austria, Hungary, and parts of other countries

casualty soldier killed or wounded in battle

Central Powers countries fighting against the Allies in World War I, including Germany, Austria-Hungary, and Turkey

civil war war fought between two sides from the same country to gain control of the country

colony land that is ruled by people from overseas

communist form of government in which all property is controlled by the government rather than individuals, and the government closely controls people's lives

conscientious objector person who refuses to fight for moral or religious reasons

conscript force all people in a group, such as all men of a certain age, to serve in the armed forces

domestic servant person who works doing cooking, cleaning, and other tasks in wealthy homes. Domestic servants were a feature of many homes before 1914.

dominion self-governing country within the British Empire, including Australia, New Zealand, and Canada during World War I

gassed attacked using poisonous gas

labour-saving something that enables a job or task to be done more quickly and easily

munitions weapons, shells, and other military equipment

prejudice unfairness or negative attitude towards something, such as against women workers or people of different races

rationing restrictions on how much of a product people can buy and use, such as rationing of food in wartime

recruit employ or seek volunteers

revolution overthrow of a government or leader, usually by force, to be replaced by someone else

shell explosive fired from large artillery or cannon

suffrage right to vote

trench ditch dug by soldiers so they can shelter from enemy fire. Trenches were widespread in the Great War, particularly on the Western Front, and trench systems became very complex.

unemployment not having a paid job to do

volunteer freely offer to do something; person who freely offers to do something

Western Front border of the territory held by the Central Powers and by the Allies in the West, where much of the fighting took place during World War I

FIND OUT MORE

BOOKS

Men, Women and Children in the First World War, Philip Steele (Wayland, 2012)
The Changing Role of Women Since 1900 (Research It!), Louise Spilsbury
(Raintree, 2010)
World War I (Eyewitness) (Dorling Kindersley, 2011)

WEBSITES

australia.gov.au/about-australia/australian-story/women-in-wartime
Women's experience in wartime Australia is explored on this website.

www.bbc.co.uk/schools/worldwarone
This BBC website for young people includes stories of men and women during
World War I.

www.spartacus.schoolnet.co.uk/Wfirst.htm
This site has lots of detailed information on women in World War I.

PLACES TO VISIT

Imperial War Museum, London and Manchester
www.iwm.org.uk
Visit the museums to see permanent collections and exhibitions telling the story
of war from 1914 to the present day.

Local museums will tell the story of World War I in your area. You may be able
to see pictures and read about where women worked and how the war affected
them.

TOPICS FOR FURTHER RESEARCH

- Look in more detail at the lives of particular women during wartime, such as
  Emmeline Pankhurst or someone less well known. You will be able to find lots
  of eyewitness accounts online.
- How has women's role in wartime changed over the last 100 years? Compare
  World War I and World War II and their impact in your area.

INDEX